PRAYING in THOUGHTS

J.T. Marshall

PRAYING in THOUGHTS

An escape route from Insomnia

J.T. Marshall

Copyright ©2017 J.T. Marshall

ISBN: 978-978-963-041-7

All rights reserved. No part of this book may be reproduced, distributed, stored in a retrieval system, or transmitted, in any form or by any means, electronic, electrostatic, magnetic tape, mechanical, photocopying, recording, or otherwise without prior written permission from the Publisher.
For information about permission to reproduce selections from this book, write to info@wrr.ng

National Library of Nigeria Cataloguing-in-Publication Data

Cover Design: Akila Jibrin

Printed and Published in Nigeria by:
Words Rhymes & Rhythm Limited
Suite C309, Global Plaza Plot 366, Obafemi Awolowo Way, Jabi District, Abuja, Nigeria.
08169027757, 08060109295
www.wrr.ng

CONTENTS

DEDICATION 7

FOREWORD 8

PART ONE 12

    UNDERSTANDING SLEEP 13

    (A sweet force) 13

    MINDING MY SLEEP 17

    UNDOING THE LID 21

    A FRESH OUTLOOK 26

    NO JUSTIFICATION 30

    NO NEGOTIATION 31

    THE RISE AGAIST INSOMNIA 33

    YOUR THOUGHTS YOUR WEAPON 41

PART TWO 45

    PRAYING IN THOUGHTS 46

    THE BASIS FOR PRAYING IN THOUGHTS 50

    ALL KINDS OF PRAYER 53

PART THREE 56

WORSHIP IN THOUGHTS 57

THANKSGIVING THROUGH PRAYING IN THOUGHTS 62

EFFICACY OF THE WORD IN PRAYING IN THOUGHTS 64

CONFESSION TO SLEEP 68

PRAYING IN THE SPIRIT THROUGH PRAYING IN THOUGHTS 71

TRANSLATE AND TRANSPORT 74

A GOOD CONSCIENCE 78

SUMMARY 82

DEDICATION

To the blessed memory of my late mother, Mrs. N. J. Tagwai (Jakkadiyan Bajju 1) and my pastor, Ina Omakwu. They inspired me to fight the good fight of faith.

FOREWORD

Being once a victim of sleeplessness and as innocent and helpless as I was, it posed as a situation that did seem insurmountable. But through unrelenting determination and dogged quest to overcome this problem, I encountered God's help. Today, I sleep with ease. Sleep does not dictate to me unlike before, rather I have it just like every normal human being. By the reason of this victory, I am bold to say, under the grace of God, that it is possible for anyone in this kind of situation to regain natural sleep.

It is no longer news that lack of sleep is prevalent among adults in the world today and unfortunately, many see it as not just a mild disorder but a terminal disease ordained for most adult. Little wonder, many shy away from taking the responsibility of facing the gruesome reality of having to live and deal with the scourge. This problem, however, has become a major factor for the ever-growing cases of drug intake and consequent addiction.

Insomnia is considered, by those who experience it, as a stigma in a way, although, I did not regard mine as such. I was rather discontented to find myself not being able to sleep when I really knew I should. I feel it is for this sole reason that I had to put myself under intense pressure to find a solution, until I was able to locate the key that unlocked the mystery which had eluded me for years and also brought a lasting solution to my predicament.

It is common knowledge that sleep is essential for healthy living, growth and development, especially for people at tender age. This was one thing that I missed for a long time. I craved for it and even more because I read in the Bible that *"...for God wants His loved ones to get their proper rest"* (Psalms 127:2 TLB).

As I struggled to believe that getting back my natural sleep was a possibility and at the time battled to reject the reality of a strange life that had for years had me seeking to sleep without artificial help, I would often ponder on this scripture and reflect why and how every effort I tried to experiment would not work in my favor.

A few years earlier, I, for some unknown reasons, refused to agree with anyone who holds the opinion that sleeplessness is normal and is naturally bestowed on some. As a matter of ill providence, I grew up to know my mother was a mild victim of lack of adequate sleep and for this reason, it was expected that the forces of hereditary was likely to take their toll on me. To a large extent, it did even though I till this day hold the opinion that the reality is just a coincidence.

This revelation, however, compelled me to keep resisting this force, which ironically resulted to losing my hold on achieving my aim of having a sound sleep. I spent long hours in bed with my eyes wide opened—unable to sleep. I kept hoping it would get better but nothing changed. Frustration was creeping in and I was forced to believe the actualization of what I had over time perceived to be an obvious superstition.

However though I was determined to break the ugly jinx by a means I know very little about. All I had was a big dream and a right thought based on Proverbs 23:7, which I had cause to memorize; "For as he thinks in his heart, so is he…"

My determination was strong and I was fully ready to undo this strange grip from my life. I remained firm on my resolve that there could be a way out of it, and so for the next few years, I did everything possible to overturn an established age-long wrong phenomenon; it was a difficult and trying period for me.

PRAYING IN THOUGHTS

PART ONE

UNDERSTANDING SLEEP

(A sweet force)

I experienced insomnia for over two decades. I labored, however, to discover a way to have my sleep back as designed. By my experience with sleeping difficulties, I have come to understand that sleep is a force. Natural sleep is therefore a positive force and it is the right of every human being to enjoy form birth till death.

This concept of force, in every ramification, is such that one needs to give proper explanation to in order to understand its semantic employment, especially in relation to the context of sleep in this book. Force, as used here, connotes a strong influence over an individual to the point of subjection to act or otherwise in a particular way, form or order. Based on this insight, I have observed that the force of natural sleep comes in two manners: it descends unaware on humans and other times, it is waited for. Although in most situations, when sleep is waited for, it does not happen according to expectation or takes time to be achieved.

As far as sleep is concerned, there are two categories of people:

PRAYING IN THOUGHTS

- Category A – those who easily fall asleep easily and naturally.
- Category B – those who find sleep difficult to achieve.

People in Category A can sleep for an average of eight hours and above, effortlessly, every night and often in the day time; whilst those in Category B would leap for joy when they can get a paltry two to three hours per night and almost impossible to sleep during the day. Those in Category A often wonder how and why Category B folks find it hard to get good sleep at will. They tend to view those with sleeping difficulties as self-inflicted or too busy and selfish with personal pursuits to care about sleep.

I remember my childhood years when I easily fell asleep in the middle of a church service despite the heavy instrumentals combined with thunderous shouts and claps of worshipers. In fact, back in those years, my mother, of blessed memory, would place her hand-bag to serve as a pillow for my head leaving the rest of my body on the bare floor of the church while I slept for several hours. At the end of most of those services, waking me up was always a huge task for her due to how deeply I would have fallen into a sleep that I did not bargain for. Where anyone would think impossible to sleep when you consider the environmental factors such as the poor structural layout of the church done without consideration for proper ventilation and the killing heat situation owing to poor nature of power supply that is prevalent in the tropical parts of Nigeria and especially when the attendance was in full capacity, yet, I slept soundly. These were never enough to disturb my normal routine of uninterrupted sleep. My mother would try to force me to stand on my feet so I could pick a lesson or two from the service but like heated butter, I would melt under the irresistible force of natural sleep. I simply and honestly could not fathom how, or what was behind this until after so many years when I ran into the problem of sleeplessness.

From personal observation, I noticed that as one develops to an adult, the rate at which one sleeps declines. In most situations, the force of natural sleep is weakened by some internal reactions in the body coupled with the influence of other external factors on the mind of the growing adult, making natural sleep seem like a scarce commodity. On the other hand, the misguided belief by many that loss of natural sleep is sometimes 'normal' for 'most adults' has resulted into the heavy dependence on sleep-inducing drugs to get a few hours of sleep. At this point, however, the innocent sufferer runs into complications and one of these is drug addiction.

MINDING MY SLEEP

For well over two decades of my life, I experienced more difficult than pleasant moments of having to live with a life of less sleep. I have earlier noted that as a growing child, I had enjoyed my great moments; I could easily get to sleep whenever I wanted.

As far as I can recollect, the process of initiating sound sleep was automatic. It was a default mechanism which required no effort on my part for sleep to be triggered. As a growing child back then, bed-wetting was regular, which till today I believe is an indication of a sound sleep and not just an annoying behavior common among growing children. Without exaggeration, I was a sleeping machine of some sort because I could take off in a flash anytime I so desired and in some cases even when I did not. In nearly all of such occasions, it would have to take a scene to get me up and steady as my mother would have to scream right directly into my ears to me back to consciousness.

I can recall a number of occasions when I slept so deeply to a level that can be equated to a 'semi coma'. Such occasions would more often than not, leave me missing out on vital lesson sessions in the classroom which may only last between 30 to 35 minutes. Sadly, at those moments, it would be an almost impossible exercise to pick a single piece of information from the lesson, all owing to an overpowering force of reoccurring bouts of the offending urge to go on sleeping the instant my back hit anything that looked like a flat surface solid enough to hold me and even in the most unlikely places.

At this point, it is quite understandable for anyone to raise the question whether I had some form of ailment caused be the popular African sleep-inducing fly, the tsetse fly, but it was nothing near it. My sleeping habit was pure and natural, a category "A" (as noted earlier) in its sharpest form.

However, as adolescence descended on me, some strange dimensions of sleep drought surfaced in my innocent life. I suddenly woke up to an experience of constant nights of endless thoughts; events and circumstances of the things I knew, the ones I didn't know and sometimes the uncertainty of what the future holds. Clearly, it then goes to show that there is a connection between the working of the mind and sleep—the mind has a very strong influence on the way one sleeps. This was as a fallout of the tones of uninvited thoughts that would always be present with me almost every night I go to bed.

During those dark days, it was not apparent to me whether or not my lack of sleep had a connection with any medical or biological disorder as I have previously speculated. Moreover, if I knew as much as I did a few years later, I probably would have found my remedy long before now. As years rolled by, the unending pursuit for better life placed so much pressure on me and my situation assumed another dimension. For instance, the pressures to make a respectable grade that could ensure admission into the university, the rigorous life of sports I found myself into was mounting, the pressing need to read for longer hours and to perform better became inevitable and all these were telling on my mind and body, hence, sleeping as at when due soon became incredibly difficult.

Adulthood did not present hope of redemption either; rather it heightened the intensity of my predicament. As it seemed then, I was faced with the threat of an imminent physical collapse due to accumulated hours of one level of less sleep to another. The need and desire to sleep by all means with the result I got day after day of less sleep took another plunge of a declining proportion. Most nights afterwards would be dreadfully unpleasant especially when there was a burning issue that required concerted reasoning which called for soundness of mind and body. Moments as such would seem like a tug of war between staying awake and getting to sleep—often, the former prevailed over the latter.

Bed-time needless thoughts compounded and to a larger extent seemed to be the culprit to my lack of sleep. These thoughts were coming in torrents—conflicting and persistent. Nights after nights turned out to be periods when I would lie in bed then unconsciously I would delve into series of mundane thoughts coming in chains and quick successions. Sometimes they would come in segments; involvements with individuals and romance with pipe dreams, aspirations of the known and the unknown within and around my little miserable world. Unfortunately, those daily tormenting routine of night thoughts would almost always leave me with long hours of soberness and irritations adding to the more torturous strain and unspeakable degree of fatigue, migraine, itchy eyes, nausea, discomfort and an increasing frustration – it was that serious.

During those trying times, the slightest contemplation of a life of sleep without sleeping pills was like the proverbial biblical camel going through the eye of the needle—it was a near hellish kind of experience—a tale of a sad case; and as desperation and despair were beginning to set in, I knew then that something would have to be done quickly in order to save the situation that seemed life-threatening.

UNDOING THE LID

Insomnia (the technical term for sleeplessness) is prevalent all over the world today and has had a lot of people held in captivity, reducing them into perpetual life of endless misery and frustrated every effort to stay healthy. Seeking for medical help, in my own experience, has only proven that medical science to solving insomnia only gives a prospect of a very distressing precedence for people to become and remain victims for as long as they live. I sometimes wonder in subjective suspicion too, whether there is a connivance between medical practitioners and pharmaceutical companies to the continued prevalence of insomnia when one considers the flourishing state in the sales of sleep-inducing drugs. This suspicion, however, is as hard to prove as it is to debunk.

More misleading than the medically proven facts surrounding the subject of insomnia is the categorisation of all people into segments of those who are prone or susceptible to be and remain victims for life even when there is no traceable evidence to convince the most naive on the matter. The classification is sadly coined in such a way that one could hardly escape finding a space to fit in one or two places within such categorisations.

Medical science researches have forced many to believe that insomnia can be caused owing to a number of reasons ranging from biological, psychological, to strong negative habits and in some cases, hereditary. As a matter of personal interest, my area of focus is not to elaborate on the causes of insomnia but to expose a distinct element that is so common to all sufferers as a channel to divine solution to it. This distinction, however, is not peculiar to a particular group of sufferers, but it is prevalent in the regular experiences of all insomnia victims. It is my humble belief that once this distinct element is unmasked, mastered and tackled, the reason or cause, however varied, would be subdued regardless of all medical postulations.

People who are victims of insomnia suffer in common from what I describe as the "restlessness of the mind at sleeping time". It is intrinsically generic irrespective of other causes that may have been attached to their inability to sleep. Ask anyone suffering from sleeping difficulty of what they do when they cannot sleep as at when due, you will discover that they spend those miserable moments struggling to either calm or tame their restless minds.

It is important to note that thought patterns may differ in the struggle with a restless mind, however, a glaring similarity also lies in the general mental activity ranging from random thoughts on business, family, relationship, and all manner of social interactions, leading from one level of lack of sleep to the other. These thought patterns also determine victim's degree of suffering from insomnia.

In my experience, I used to think my case as the most miserable. As far as I can recall, I was always plagued by a sudden restlessness of the mind for countless nights. Funny enough, thoughts that would normally have me held down are mostly bothered on trivialities—such that I consider as vain; dealings of the previous days, weeks or even years, which are as needless as that of the future. My efforts to arrest and subject this problem was far beyond my control because I was oblivious of where to find help. The truth is that such moments can take dimensions in terms of transition from one thought to another.

In typical situations, my transitions were always quick and successive; from one to the next—pleasant and unpleasant ones. For example, in a moment, I could lay in bed as I prepare to sleep, and could instantly begin to fantasize myself standing on stage and speaking to a group of friends or colleagues in the office or church on an idea I want them to buy into and suddenly see the entire group screaming in affirmation and apparent acceptance of the idea. I would in such a situation feel elated—a kind of an untold excitement. I may also find myself in a reckless spending spree in supermarket or a car mart. However, on returning to myself, the sudden realization that they were all figments of my usually vain imaginations, anger and frustration would set in ultimately abandoning me into a further state of sleeplessness in a single night and the chain would continue.

Sometimes, the mind of the sufferer is plunged into thoughts which would come and go, abandoning him or her in a vacuum without a definite recollection of any substance of his or her wanderings. This is yet another mysterious type of burden many sufferers carry much to their suffering. As I gradually but desperately sought freedom from a life that seemed as though hope was forever lost, I, fortunately and for reasons I cannot fully grasp, held a belief that it was possible to have a natural way out of the predicament.

As I persistently nursed my dream for redemption, the question of how to deal with my ever working mind became very central. I was, in the actual sense, disturbed in my contemplations since the solution to its remedy seemed farfetched. Notwithstanding, I kept my dreams and hopes alive not for any particular reason other than to know that at least someday, somehow, something would happen for my desired liberation.

The fact was that the feeling of such prospects brought hope and a bit of relief to my ever growing predicament. Through the power of a burning desire to break free, I pictured that my reoccurring bouts of restlessness when in bed could be altered with the application of the right methods. I initially found out that the root of my ordeal was not when my mind is made up to sleep but rather when I am anxious to get sleep even when I am hardly prepared for it. As it was always the case, each time I allowed that to happen, desperation would leave my chances to sleep battered for that night and several others for as long as having the right state of mind remained elusive.

Without any fear of contradiction, I was able to figure out that my experience of sleeplessness was caused by a gamut of confused mental and psychological state of mind and as a matter of fact, a self-inflicted phenomenon that was increasingly tough to contest.

A FRESH OUTLOOK

A glimpse into the power of a mindset will usher us into a world of limitless possibilities where insomnia is involved. As a matter reality, it can make or break you, determine you excel or otherwise. Your thoughts which form your mindset can make you feel powerful or powerless, a victim or a victor. In our material life, our thoughts can make us a success or a bunch of failures. Our thoughts, and the actions that they trigger, determine our whole life including our sleep. And the best news of all is that they are completely under our own control.

The fact that you and I can think, reflect and so often regret the past, imagine and so often fear the future, seem to be a blessing. However, these abilities could also be used to rob us of some of life's best gifts, especially the way we perceive insomnia and the mindset many of us carry about it as part of our daily lifestyles.

If you must succeed at consistently having your normal sleep, it remains imperative to bear in mind that you deserve a wonderful life, full of success, happiness, joy, and excitement. You are entitled to have happy and excellent health, meaningful work life, and freedom to exercise all your God given abilities to the fullest. These are your birthright. This is what your life is meant to encompass. You are engineered for success and designed to have high levels of self-fulfillment. You must come to that place of accepting that you have absolutely amazing untapped ability that can regenerate natural sleep. The only real limits on what you can be, do, or have are the limits you place on yourself by your own mind set.

You have to have a new perspective about your future, sleep and life which must be abundantly unlimited. Each person comes into the world with no thoughts or ideas at all, and everything that a person thinks and feels is learned from infancy onward. The adult becomes the sum total of everything he or she learns, feels, and experiences growing up. What the adult does and becomes later is majorly the result of this early conditioning.

In every case, if you want to change your performance and your results in any area of your life and especially on getting back your natural sleep, you have to change your self-concept—or your beliefs about yourself—as one who can recover and have a normal sleep life.

Fortunately, our beliefs are largely subjective. They are not always based on the reality. Instead, they are based largely on our thinking taken in and accepted as true, sometimes with very little evidence or proof. The very worst beliefs you can have are self-limiting beliefs of any kind. These are beliefs about yourself that cause us to feel somehow limited or deficient. These beliefs are seldom true, but if you accept them as valid estimates of your ability, they become true for you, exactly as if they are correct. The starting point of unlocking your potential, and accomplishing more than you ever have before, is for you to challenge your self-limiting beliefs. You begin this process of freeing yourself from self-limiting beliefs by acknowledging that whatever they are, they are completely untrue. Imagine for the moment that you have no limitations on your abilities at all.

There are several myths that we accept as we grow up that can sabotage our opportunity for success, joy, good sleep and fulfillment later in life. Let's look at one of those self-limiting beliefs one at a time. The first for the supposed victim of insomnia is summarized in the feeling, "I'm not good enough to have my sleep anymore." This is the basic premise that causes feelings of inferiority and inadequacy. We assume that other people are better than we are just because, at the moment, they are doing better with sleep than we are. Therefore, we must be worth less than them.

This feeling of worthlessness which insomnia generates sits deep in the psyche and causes us to sell ourselves short and eliminate our vision of seeing the possibilities of getting everything reversed in all the unfortunate circumstances surrounding our lack of sleep.

NO JUSTIFICATION

Justification here is what you do when you rationalize or create a reason for your frustration caused by lack of sleep. You tell yourself and to whoever cares to listen to you how badly and dreadfully unfair life has been for you and maybe how unbothered you are about the problem or how your ancestors are behind your predicament. You repeat all the reasons you have for being upset with why you have to remain a victim. Each time you think of the situation, you privately become angry and hopeless. You feel entitled to your anger. However, as if you have paid a high price for it, especially since, in your estimation, you were such an innocent victim.

The way you short-circuit the natural tendency towards justification and rationalization is by refusing to engage in it. Instead, you have to stop justifying. You use your marvelous mind to think of reasons not to justify your negative emotions. Remember, your negative emotions do you no good. They are totally destructive and further scuttle your chances of overcoming insomnia. They do not affect the other person or change the situation. They simply undermine your happiness and self-confidence and peace, making you weaker and less effective in other areas of your life as I spent most of my past life with insomnia.

NO NEGOTIATION

Like in a battle, people have little or no room at all for initiating a plan for a renegotiation for withdrawal once the incursion begins. This was the mental attitude I had when I approached insomnia. I found within me, the zest to step out headlong to tackle the situation regardless of some "lurked inside" skepticism – for I had my fair share; as every human being, it would be mischievous to conceal my past travails from insomnia by contemplating anything that could suggest physically or psychologically unharmed by sleeplessness as this would only have simply betrayed weakness and lack of sincerity.

My fear, approaching the threshold of wading into battle against insomnia, was not unfounded; this is largely because I was stepping into an area I suppose was strange to me. Aside this peculiar kind of skepticism, I did not envisage nor was I prepared to entertain any form of failure. However, when my mind was made as to delve completely into seeking a permanent solution, the task of doing away with my fears became somewhat simple to the extent I still wonder if I had ever entertained one in the first place.

Having crossed that huddle, I knew that I needed to come to a place where I could see my journey as one that was void of a retreat plan.

I had to discard all fears of ever bearing in mind that the adventure could in any way fail to deliver.

As we confront insomnia, our attitude towards this war should be total.

Paul spoke about this attitude at the end of 1 Corinthians 15. He was explaining to the Christians in Corinth that the bodily resurrection is the sign of our victory over death and Satan. That victory is already guaranteed through the resurrection of Jesus Christ, but only if we don't give in. In one of the great verses of the Bible, Paul wrote,

"Therefore, my beloved brethren, be steadfast, immovable, always abounding in the work of the Lord, knowing that your labor is not in vain in the Lord."
(1 Cor. 15:58 KJV)

Consider the import of Paul's words. He uses two synonymous terms to describe this "never give in" attitude: steadfast and immovable. Stead comes from an Old English word meaning place or position. So the idea behind being steadfast is that you hold your ground. You stand firm. You don't give in. The victim that will gain the victory in the end is the one who does not waver from what is right regardless of the temptation or persecution. Immovable is similar in thought. No matter what comes, we must be unassailable and unshakable.

THE RISE AGAINST INSOMNIA

"Jesus said, if there are no 'ifs' among believers. Anything can happen'" (Mark 9:23 MSG)

My life experience with insomnia was like that of a drowning man struggling to find something to lay hold on to survive. I was left with almost nothing but an unflinching desire to break free. I refused to accept that insomnia is normal by any justification. By a strange prompting, I knew that I could break free and get my sleep without necessarily being induced by drugs. Vehemently, I held within that if sleeplessness comes as natural, it could be done away with in the same manner. I took my stand firmly in the scriptural words of (Mark 10:27 NKJV)

> *"And Jesus looking upon them saith, with men it is impossible, but not with God: for with God all things are possible."*

These words again reinforced the hope for possible victory and formed the cornerstone for what would turn out to be a massive breakthrough from my unpleasant experience. As my ability to sleep continued to degenerate, I was determined to believe even the more, that a natural remedy exists somewhere. As a matter of fact, I soon began to seek ways in order to find my escape route.

Suffice it to say that it was embarrassing at first to realize that as a person, I was made a victim by aligning myself to a popular myth. I had also been vulnerable by allowing my mind to become a breeding ground for all kinds of unnecessary beliefs. Having realized this, I kept the zest to fight the problem to the last. Taking it personal, I knew deep inside of me that I needed to come to terms with the glaring reality of what was against me. I was concerned with how to crack the mystery of insomnia as a challenge. Again, I reasoned that if I failed to put up a strong fight against this monster, I never would experience sleeping naturally till death. This fact spurred me into further determination to rise and fight to finish the experience of living with this dreaded disorder.

The story behind my freedom from sleeplessness has its roots from my experience of God as a growing child in the wake of the early 90s; I had been privileged to be a bit ardent in the study of the Bible; this I owe to the solid foundation my mother had laid for me at a tender age. Back then, it was mandatory for everyone in the family to attend the regular morning and evening family altars—a daily routine that no one dared to miss. Sunday school was also another compulsory ritual for every member of the family. These two formed the basis for a habit that was later to develop into a love for reading the Bible–something I initially considered as a pastime.

Back to the unpleasant days of my depressing sleeplessness and the desperate quest to break free, having consented to taking responsibility, I delved, as a matter of necessity, into seeking to know the scriptural stance concerning my worsening sleeping condition. This I did with the hope that my remedy might spring out miraculously, hence, I did an intensive study of the scripture. This effort led me to yet another life transforming scripture found in (Hebrews 1:3 MSG)

*"... and is stamped with God's nature. He holds **everything** together by what he says – powerful words!"*

It was again more delightful to find out that EVERYTHING responds to the word of God. I then began to believe the possibility of a positive return of my natural state of sleep that had been negatively altered for more than two decades ~~by insomnia~~. Consequently, I continued in the word of God and as I persisted in its meditation, God revealed more unto me. I discovered again that it would be impossible to earn or appropriate ANY blessing on earth from the LORD without FAITH according to (Hebrews 11:6 GNT).

"No one can please God without faith, for whosoever comes to God must have faith that God exist and reward those who seek Him."

The more I studied the scriptures, the more my faith grew in God. I began to see myself laying hold on whatever I so desire to have only if I dared to BELIEVE with the eyes of my mind. My eyes were opened and I felt a deep conviction within that I was finally breaking free from my growing insomnia. This brought a kind of inner joy in no small measure into my spirit —a ray of hope at last was in view. I became more deeply attached to the study of God's word with faith and I was made to discover how amazing the word of God is. Through the study of the word of God, I discovered that:

- Sleep is a natural gift of God and is not bound to be interrupted throughout one's lifetime.
- Sleep-inducing drugs are not part of the plan of God for His children.
- In the case of sleeplessness, to regain the normal state of sleep is possible without external aids.
- Human beings have dominion over sleep and not the other way round.

With these newly found understanding, I prayerfully began to engage myself in a frantic battle with my problem of sleeplessness. I was from then on helped to launch into the discovery of a divine solution to my case. By the privilege of revelation, I was opened to several other scriptures that created in me the power to overcome sleeplessness. Permit me to quickly state here that the immediate impact the application of these verses had on me completely rendered all my artificial sleeping aids useless.

Not only that the potency of the word of God liberated me from the dependence on sleep-inducing aids but also changed my thought on sleeping difficulties as caused by whatever "known" factors such as hereditary, fatigue effects, body type, anxiety, diets etc. as a mere pretext for suppressing the effect of insomnia to its victims. The truth is, they all failed in the test of the infallible word of God which is over and above all sources of knowledge. However, I do not want us to be ignorant of the fact that one or a few of these sources may actually contribute to prolonging an already established sleeping problem. What I am trying to establish is that they could NEVER have been the cause at the onset.

In one of my revelations, I discovered that every attempt done by a child of God to gain liberty from challenges is always hindered, one way or the other, by an opposing force which stems from Lucifer (the devil). He is the fallen Angel who rebelled against the sovereignty of God. It is recorded in the Bible that:

"The thief (Devil) comes not, but for to steal, and to kill, and to destroy; I am

come that they may have life, and that they might have it more abundantly." *(John 10:10 KJV)*

Note here that the enemy is desperate to take away anything that gives us comfort and one of such is our gift of sound sleep. However, gaining ABUNDANT LIFE (a life of completeness) can only be accessed under a condition, hence the word "might" in the above scripture. This implies a personal responsibility of constantly placing the Devil where he belongs and choice to enjoy the blessings packaged by God for our lives.

We must not be ignorant of the fact that what we see in the physical is the resultant effect of what has been completed in the spiritual. Therefore, it is God's desire for his children to enjoy continuous sound sleep. The Bible reminds us of this in the book of Psalms:

"I will both lie down and sleep in peace; for you alone O LORD make me lie down in safety." (Psalm 4:8 NRSV)

"It is vain to rise up early, to sit up late, to eat the bread of sorrows: for so he giveth His beloved sleep." (Psalm 127:2 KJV)

As God's children, we are required to continually resist the enemy (the one who steals and destroys our sleep) and to take back whatever he must have stolen from us. The Bible instructs us in (James 4:7 KJV)

> "*Submit yourselves therefore to God. Resist the devil, and he shall flee from you.*"

May I say here that my liberation from insomnia is a testimony and a fulfilment of these scriptures; the remedy I found which changed my sleep life is a classic case of resisting the Devil. My experience of sleeping difficulty taught me one important lesson; to vehemently refuse to accept undesirable circumstances even if the general notion of overcoming is on the negative. I consistently did not fail to maintain a solid positive mental stance of overcoming it, and it came to pass.

During the time my condition grew worse back then, when I would stay awake for 48 hours and beyond, struggling to get just a little sleep but to no avail. Eventually I would have no other choice but to give in to sleeping inducers, yet, I was not deterred by what I faced. I confidently maintained the notion that my condition was not without a remedy. Each passing experience came with so much frustration accompanied with myriads of random thoughts and mundane concerns. Still, I guarded my heart with faith under God against the thought of impossibility and the pressure my condition was having on me. I continued to refuse the idea of being a defeated victim.

I see my testimony of liberation set a channel of miracle for others who are victims that through the help of this book will also achieve the same victory I achieved over my situation. I must confess that my earnest seeking for a lasting solution to my past condition opened me into a revelation of divine help which brought an end to my predicament. I overcame! You can too!

YOUR THOUGHTS YOUR WEAPON

"Casting down imaginations, and every high thing that exalteth itself against the knowledge of God, and bringing into captivity every thought to the obedience of Christ."
(II Corinthians 10:5 KJV)

Bed-time for victims of insomnia can be one of the most dreaded moments of their daily lives; there is always a mixture of anxiety and tension. In my experience of these frustrated moments, I sometimes had to rely on chances to hit the blank memory point in order to get sleep without the aid of sleeping pills and sometimes, especially when my situation aggravated, to achieve sleep as a fall back of prolonged lack of regular sleep and stress caused by the restlessness of mind. In such occasions, I would be left with no other choice but to resort to the use of even more powerful sleep inducing pills on a constant basis. However having meditated on the above passage of the bible, I had an inkling that the enemy was playing some pranks with my mind and I needed to get him out as soon as possible

During those days of my pain and desperation, I experimented various lying positions and discovered that I was a bit more relaxed and recorded some easy sleep moments especially when I lie down on my belly rather than on my side or on my back. Interestingly, I also discovered that it reduce fatigue and my uncontrollable flow of thoughts during bed time. Unfortunately, this discovery did not last long. I soon returned to my experience of sleeplessness and a hard time warring with thoughts on my mind no matter how I tried to maintain a particular sleeping position for prolong periods of time. It rather became clearer to me that beside the task of putting my body positioning and ensuring it remained motionless, the reoccurring thoughts and the challenge to keep the body transfixed was even more tiring. I was then caught up between focusing on working on my body positions and the unwanted thoughts. In all these, I was glad I discovered for the first time at least, something had shifted; there is a glimmer of hope.

By this experience, it was obvious to me that sleeping position (flat on the belly) and especially if I can keep my body still for a good number of minutes could help induce sleep but cannot tackle the challenge of my ever restless mind. I always had a fierce battle with the myriads of thoughts that came on my mind whenever I'm in bed. It was the stumbling block to my sleep and it turned out to be even more increasingly tough to keep calm.

I realized through divine help that what my eyes saw were also a contributing factor on the thoughts that occupied my mind. Anytime I went to bed, I would gaze round the room unconsciously trying to focus on a thing or two to ponder on. As I reflect on the past, I cannot vividly recall how long I had spent precious time sighting objects which automatically drew me into thoughts and at the same time taking my mind away from focusing on sleep. That instant, I would roam at random, the world of wild thoughts on events, items and objects. While I stayed on those vain distractions, unconsciously, I would feel an intense soberness setting in my spirit and these could last for countless hours.

But then in all these, like I have emphasized earlier in a previous chapter, I persisted in a deep study of the word of God and something strange happened as I began to listen to the still voice in my spirit. It was during this period that I got a revelation to what brought a lasting solution to my situation.

The thoughts that occupied my mind during bed-time became an area of concentration. I figured out the thoughts on my mind were responsible for my captivity in the hands of insomnia. I reasoned that my thoughts could also be used to produce the much needed link to recover my lost ability to get sleep if divinely directed. From that moment on, I needed nobody to tell me that a redirection was possible and that was where my victory story began.

With everything in perspective, I then shifted my focus to where I could hinge my strength on; the fact that I have been given the ability to "cast down" (by implication, to do away with) and to "bring into captivity" (being lord over) all unwanted thoughts. Therefore, I decided that if there was a man that had the need to speedily witness the manifestation of these words of God, it was certainly I.

The revelation of the truth in the word of God made a significant difference not only on the fact that my thoughts which had, over the years, made me a captive of sleeplessness can be divinely directed and bring about an assured liberation without external aids but also on my entire being as I continued to rely on Him for help.

PART TWO

PRAYING IN THOUGHTS
(The Master Key)

"And it came to pass, as she continued praying before the LORD, that Eli marked her mouth.

Now Haanah, she spake with her heart; only her lips moved, but her voice was not heard: therefore Eli thought she had been drunken.

And Eli said to her, how long wilt thou be drunken? Put away thy wine from thee.

And Hannah answered and said, No, my lord, I am a woman of a sorrowful spirit; I have drunk neither wine nor strong drink, but have poured my soul before the LORD.

Wherefore it came to pass, when time was come about after Hannah had conceived, that she bare a son, and called his name Samuel, saying, because I have asked him of the LORD."

(1samuel 1:12-15, 20 kjv)

My victory over insomnia came when I took another form of communication with God which, by the reason of experience, I can confidently say that it works miracle. My spiritual eyes were opened to what I call "Praying in Thoughts". It should interest anyone to examine the prayer style a barren Hannah made to "call forth" Prophet Samuel. This opened up a model which miracles of any kind can be drawn through the mysterious hands of the Almighty God in the affairs of men.

"Praying in Thoughts" is a channel of communing with God without necessary uttering words; a communication in prayers in one's mind. This may at first sound foolish and would seem almost impossible or far from reality as this was the case with me initially. This medium of prayer was what I discovered, learnt and consistently practised until it became a second nature when I sought God to deal with my problem of insomnia. This is not saying or rendering praying verbally ineffective, rather it is another eye-opener to the workings of God in mysterious ways as a channel of blessings and miracles for our lives.

Divinely redirecting thoughts that hold our minds restless into constructive prayers helps to restore one's lost peace as a victim makes all the difference. It is important to say that this act, when fervently practiced, one will, in no time, get used to it. By this discovery, whenever I found my mind restless at bed-time and the thoughts kept pouring in, I redirected those thoughts into prayers, which sometimes could take me up to 45 minutes—uninterrupted—till I would unconsciously fall asleep at ease.

"Praying in Thoughts" was the clincher that liberated me from the over two decades of misery and pains of my life in the hands of sleeplessness. I find it expedient also to share that the concept of "Praying in Thoughts" has also immensely helped me to cast all my desires that may want to bother my mind unto God.

I know someone may want to ask why prayer, or what is this kind of prayer and how is such done? These questions and several others would be explained in detail in the subsequent chapters of this book. It is my belief that the Holy Spirit will expand this mystery in the life of every reader. And for anyone reading this book who may be suffering from insomnia in one way or the other or just as it was in my situation, I encourage you to be at ease because this is the set time for your freedom. Believe and set your mind on God—in the confidence that through this book you will also be launched into your miracle.

I feel that for a better direction on this divinely-revealed line of prayer, there is a need to properly re-examine in a bid to understand the apostle Paul's words in his second letter to the church in Corinthian where he encouraged the church to get a proper control of their thoughts by casting down every imagination that is not needed and also bringing into subjection the once that would not obey the form of which they are by creation (the way God has designed them to be).

Of a note, it is that the heart is instrumental to the experiences of humans— be it good or bad. Therefore, "Praying in Thoughts" is done in the heart. It was where I competed and conquered the contending forces militating against my ability to get sleep. Beyond insomnia, Proverbs 4:23 portrays the heart as a ground of contention for good and evil and for this sole reason we are enjoined to "guard it with all diligence".

"Keep vigilant over your heart: that is where life starts." (Proverbs 4:23 MSG)

The emphasis in the above Bible verse is what goes on in the heart—the thoughts of good life and bad life— and this earnestly calls for not only praying over our thoughts but also "Praying in Thoughts".

THE BASIS FOR PRAYING IN THOUGHTS

The infallible word of God has made it impossible to miss this open invitation to unburden whatever situation that may have defied solution. A careful study of I Peter 5:7 brings this to light. My contact with this very verse of the scripture brought about a rare illumination. The word of God there reads;

"Casting all your care upon him; for He cares for you." (I Peter 5:7NKJV)

It happened on a night after a tedious day at work, I tried to catch some sleep. I lay in bed frustrated and unable to sleep. I turned times without number, change positions but to get sleep was to no avail. To worsen the case, apart from the fact that my mind was burdened with thoughts of doubts, worries, fears and concerns. My heart pounded harder and harder at every passing minute. Anxiety set in and my emotions were twisted into a mangled mess of panic.

In the past, when my wife would notice a similar scene playing out, she would not do much than to tell me to quit worrying. I would only get angry that she wasn't worrying with me! That night, I got up, walked down to my study, I opened my Bible and I Peter 5:7 jumped at my face. I had read this verse countless times, but that night was completely a different experience. The revelation of each word was refreshing. I read again and again. What I found out from those words changed my perception and set me free from further worry and anxiety. It liberated me from carrying the burden that I had thought I could fix by myself. It reinforced my confidence in the word of God and revealed to me that my thoughts (if cast on the Lord) were channels to regain my inability to get sleep. I understood that God was interested in taking care of my problems and there was no need to put up a personal fight against my challenges. It was evident to me that by the authority of the word of God I was already an overcomer.

In a further study on the verse, I discovered that "casting" as used in I Peter 5:7 from the Greek word 'epiripto'; a compound of the words 'epi' and 'ripto'. The word 'epi' means upon, as on top of something while the word 'ripto' means to hurl, to throw, or to cast and it often means to violently throw or to fling something. The only other place the word 'epiripto' was used is in Luke 19:35, I found there that:

"*And brought him to Jesus: and they cast their garments upon the colt, and they set Jesus there on.*"

It is crucial to note that the above passage aptly conveys the idea of the word *'epiripto'*, which in secular literature is often pictured as the flinging of weights off the shoulders of a traveler and unto the back of some other beast of burden; such as donkeys, camels or horses. Ultimately, I discovered that we are not designed to carry the burden of worry, fret and anxiety. They are too much a burden than the strength of humans can bear. We may be able to bear it for a while, but eventually it will break us, just like in my experience when I was completely broken under the perpetual pressure of insomnia.

On the other hand, I also found out the word "cares", as used in I Peter 5:7, is from the Greek word 'merimna', which means anxieties (which by extension can be described as afflictions, difficulties, hardships, misfortunes, troubles or complicated circumstances) that arise as a result of problems that really bother on our general lives as individuals. Such was my predicament before a divine-intervention surfaced.

As I continued to wait on the Lord and meditate on this same verse, my weakness was revealed. I saw that I was weak and the burden I was trying to lift was beyond what my strength could carry. I saw Jesus telling me to make Him my beast of burden, that I should take my burden and heave it with my last strength on His back. And Yes! I did!

ALL KINDS OF PRAYER

"And pray in the Spirit on all occasions with ALL KINDS of prayer and request..." (Ephesians 6:18.NIV)

The encounter with the truth in the word of God is a mighty testimony to my case. The truth is that the assurance of the word of God is capable of bringing about supernatural changes to any situation that may have surpassed human comprehension.

I undertook a yet intensive study of the Bible in a bid to search for more light— truth— for the restoration of my loss. I developed great faith that it was possible to regain my ability to get sleep without any stress. Each time I searched the scriptures, I was convinced to believe that the word of God has the potential to counter my troubling thoughts and overcome insomnia. I searched even deeper. I found out that through the proper kind of prayers anything termed "impossible" is just a word.

Having received quite a number of blessings through prayer in the past, I knew that nothing can fail if I prayed right. The challenge that I battled with was the kind of prayer I needed to introduce to tackle my distressing situation. After some months of waiting on the word of God, it was finally revealed to me; and that is, "Praying in Thoughts".

As children of God, we are from time to time faced with challenges that are beyond our abilities. In such situations, we engage in different kinds of prayer in a bid to find a way out. I found myself in this situation; in a dire need of a special kind of prayer. And when I was opened to this, it was like a dream. In reality, I was glad that God opened my eyes to see this and also gave me the grace to share it. I reasoned also that if our God is multi-faceted in nature, praying to Him can and should be multi-dimensional.

One thing about prayer is that it is not limited by time. It is what to be done "without ceasing" as instructed in the scriptures in 1 Thessalonians 5:17. The truth of this then is that, if we are ever going to fulfil this scripture, it is our responsibility through the leading of the Spirit to discover other avenues of communicating with God other than the conventional way, that is, verbal prayers which many consider to be the only way to communicate with God.

As much as I did not feel troubled in my spirit about "Praying in Thoughts" as another way of communicating our desires unto God, it was a challenge for me to completely fall in line in terms of what it would take. But, because it was a leading, I had no any other choice. I see "Praying in Thoughts" as one of the "all kinds of prayer" instructed by God through the mouth of Apostle Paul in Ephesians 6:18.

Permit me to share with you that praying from within is also a potentially active tool to ask and receive from God. The know-how of this act of prayer is a jewel of miracles that liberated me from the fetters of insomnia.

PRAYING IN THOUGHTS

PART THREE

WORSHIP IN THOUGHTS

"Speaking to yourselves in psalms and hymns and spiritual songs, making melody in your heart to the Lord." (Ephesians 5:19 KJV)

As long as it is possible to pray in thoughts, it is possible also to worship in thoughts. I always began praying in my thoughts with worship making, which is, making melody in my heart. At first, it sounded ridiculous to me as much as I felt it could not yield anything but through meditation and understanding of the word of God, I was so sure of the blessing therein. I found my worshiping in thoughts as an assurance of sound sleep. Needless to say, Apostle Paul was not being unnecessarily superstitious when he said "speaking to yourselves", and also "...making melody in your heart to the Lord" in Ephesians 5:19, he spoke concerning sacrifices offered from the within the heart according to the inspiration of God—and of a truth, he was right on point. I did it and it has become my remedy to sleep.

To worship in thoughts is one type of prayer that can be introduced when one prays in thoughts—as these are forms of communing with God be it through prayers, intercessions, thanksgiving and supplications (worship) as instructed by the word of God;

> *"I exhort therefore that, first of all, supplications, prayer, intercessions and thanks be made..."* (1 Timothy 2:1 KJV)

To position oneself for the blessings in these acts of communion with God, one needs to be focused because there are challenges one can be faced with not to talk of the temptation to quit when our prayers may be interfered by the subtle creeping in of some unsolicited thoughts. In my experience, to worship in thoughts was not something I had a smooth headway with even with the revelation in place. I remember how I used to get frustrated by conflicting thoughts in my head which would surge up to disrupt an ongoing melody in my heart unto God. I was not also ignorant of the enemy's efforts to truncate whatever blessing God's children are entitled to enjoy; I had to keep on fighting to take what belongs to me.

Bringing my mind, soul and body together was such a difficult task. This happened because my mind was always suddenly preoccupied with my problem of sleeplessness and consequently, my chance of getting sleep would sometimes be interrupted. But then, with time, I was able to achieve focus through sustained practice under God. The key, here, is persistency. I would sustain the worship in my heart until I would be carried away unexpectedly by sleep.

Permit me to stress here that praying or worshiping in thoughts does not just happen by chance. It is deliberately learned and practised before one would start to enjoy of the blessing thereof. I know from experience that it is the dream point of everyone who always labour to sleep naturally to regain the ability without external aids and why I am sharing this is because of the tendency of giving up when one begins to face challenges in the course of practicing these acts of communion with God in overcoming insomnia.

One does not need to give up and like I said earlier on, persistence is the key and getting ones' entire being deeply inclined in the process. Let me also add here that a revelation can at times be received in its raw or inexplicit form from above but it behooves on the recipient-through divine wisdom to fine-tune such a blessing in order to access the real value therein.

When I worship in thoughts, I communicate with God in my heart through songs of praise and worship. It is a session that I begin with supplications—such that I view as a way of humbling myself in His presence. This time, my thoughts are keyed into a prayer for mercy from all wrongs of the day (for the Bible says in Psalms 66:18, "if I regard iniquity in my heart, the Lord will not hear me"), after which, I will utter an Amen in a form of a hum which is a type of an AMEN.

Humming is my invention which is typified by a slightly faint sound I let out (from within with my mouth shut). It is that type of sound you hear from people when a sweet sensation hits their sense of taste signaling delight and a sense of satisfaction.

This hum serves as a springboard as well as the modulator of worship session (and in all other praying in thought remedy) in my heart in the course of my praying in thoughts and so, after each worship song, I would make a conscious release of the faint hum as a seal of a consummated communion with my maker. The function of the hum is diverse. It serves as a link between one prayer point or song stanza to another, it is the first sign the man or woman gets as sleep approaches. An attempt to fully understand its workings may be hard to explain. The hum is better experienced than to analyze –

it is also one of the mysterious blessings contained in the package.

I do not hold any preference in selection of the songs I sing when I worship. The tempo with which I handle each song also varies. Sometimes, the tempo could be slower than how the song is in its default form, other times, I could take it as it is. May I add that, lowering tempo of worship songs lures the mind from wondering and makes it more comforting to get my sleep at an accelerated degree. As I persist in worship, I soon will sense an interference in the flow of my (worship in thoughts) and then notice a disruption to in humming as I gradually give in to sleep; my body generally succumbing to a strange weakness as I maintain my favorite sleeping position and make sure I remain still. At other times, I would slowly fall into a state of dizziness; an assurance that sleep is imminent which I will always welcome with gratitude.

Of a note, praying in thoughts or worshiping in thoughts are not just means to overcome sleeplessness. I see these acts of communion as real services unto God in themselves, just like every conventional way of prayer and worship—a sacrifice of faith—a possession of every sound child of God. The signal of delight and satisfaction that follows is completely overwhelming.

THANKSGIVING THROUGH PRAYING IN THOUGHTS

Permit me to share one very important aspect of prayer that I cherish so much. *The prayer of thanksgiving*. I must admit that this helped me immensely in my liberation. There were nights I became so burdened with certain distractions and unable to get quick sleep and on such occasions, I would quickly redirect my thoughts into unending words of appreciation (a plethora of things to be thankful for).

I had different transitional markers such as 'I am grateful...', "I cannot forget to give thanks for...", "I give thanks for..." and a host of others as I transited in my thoughts of thanksgiving. I usually did (and still do) this in order to keep my mind on track and not giving in to the pressure of worthless thoughts.

In my prayer of thanksgiving, typically, I would go on mentioning in my thoughts the names of everyone in my family from my immediate to extended members marked by a seal of thankfulness and this could take up to 10- 15 minutes. At other times, I would go on mentioning all the people I had come across in a day or the previous one, the activities in the office, the outcomes of events of the same day. Midway into my paying, my previously restless mind would have been streamlined to dwell on trying to only remember who or what next to be thankful for. I would also not forget maintain my favorite sleeping position and make sure I remain still. There, I would go on to list countless stuffs, completely enthralled with my mind weighed down by the activity, and before long, I would be fast asleep. The manner at which sleep happens on me when all these are put in place is still phenomenal to me.

The simple act of giving thanks is a blessing on its own and little wonder why the Bible, through the mouth of Apostle Paul, enjoins us to render our supplications "in thanksgiving". I consider my act of praying in thoughts by giving thanks as another unique way of mine to fulfil this scriptural requirement in (Ephesians 5:20 GNT) *"in the name of our Lord Jesus Christ, always giving thanks for everything to God the Father"*

Since this experience, I have come to understand that there is a great reward in showing appreciation for both small and big blessings that I receive each day from God and I do not joke with it – I am always sincerely grateful!

EFFICACY OF THE WORD IN PRAYING IN THOUGHTS

"This book of the law shall not depart from your mouth; but you shall meditate on it day and night." (Joshua 1:8 KJV)

The effectiveness of the word of God in liberating people from all forms of bondages cannot be overemphasized. As I journeyed through my converted experience with sleep through Thanksgiving and worship, there came a time when I pondered an idea of how my sleep life could be if I had a variety of ways to call my sleep as often as I wish and have it obliged me, then another miracle struck. Just like in the conventional way of praying to God, by reciting the God's word back to HIM; however in my own thoughts works great miracles. And of course, this is also one of the means by which anyone can achieve sleep.

If I must say, praying is a serious business and this is why when it is done, it is must not be done with head knowledge (as a matter of fact, such does not have much effect). It is worthy to reiterate again that my previous knowledge of the word that nothing is impossible for God to overturn made every other thing attainable even in the face of contrary physical evidence. The dimension of faith I received from the life in it settled my doubts. I now know that all things can rise and fall by the power in the word of God. I know by the power of God I have forever overcome insomnia.

Armed with my latest discovery, my subsequent romance and the coveted style of prayer, there was no need for hesitation as I hurriedly gathered most of the scriptures I know that speak of God's promise of freedom, did an in-depth study of them and committed them to my memory.

While in bed, restless, I would begin reciting them in my mind as I would in my prayer. And yes! I did pray through. A point worthy of note here is the fact that I would unrelentingly keep repeating the recitation of these scriptures (in my thoughts) over and over until the expected happens.

Some of my few favorite freedom verses are:

"So If the Son set you free, you are free through and through" (John 8:36 MSG)

> *"Since he did not spare even his own son for us but gave him up for us all, won't he also surely give us everything else?"* (Romans 8:32 TLB)

> *"We have not received this world's Spirit; instead, we have we have the Spirit sent by God, so that we may know ALL that God has given us."* (I Corinthians 2:12 GNT)

> *"Stand fast therefore in the liberty Christ had made us FREE, and be not entangled again with the yoke of bondage."* (Galatians 5:1 KJV)

Just like faith, freedom is also a force that we need to see with the eyes of our minds as a gift that can be received and with the assurance that we have truly been free from all forms of what we detest even when all the evidences of such assurances are not visible. The discovery, meditation and application of these verses brought contrary evidences to the voices of impossibilities in my life.

Freedom is one thing that everyone who is under the scourge of any unfortunate situation should seek and embrace in order to enjoy the miracles that come with it and the first step to be free is to believe that one is free. As a child of God, you need to understand that every man has been given the liberty to know ALL THINGS that are FREELY given. I made bold to say once again that it was through the power of the word of God, I received my freedom from insomnia.

By revelation, I came to see that by meditating on the word day and night, I can have all my ways prosperous and achieve a good success. This promise also covers the recovery of all losses. I coveted more of intensive meditations of the word of God and the more I did, the greater insight and wisdom I encountered with regard to getting back my sleep in my new ways. Need I say here again that the joy of knowing the word of God and how much its works in my strange situation is immensely valuable. And there, I began to see my praying in thoughts also as a form of meditation.

As I look back, it is almost impossible not to recall the elation which surges through my heart every day I wake up to see how these words had brought about a turning point to my life. My challenge of sleeplessness gave way and by just merely reciting from my heart; not just by quoting them and consistently engaging my favorite hum after each repeated verse by drawing the truth and blessing contained in them and relying on the Spirit of God to harness the power and life therein blessed me.

"...*The words that I speak to you are spirit, and they are life.*" (John 6:63 KJV)

Therefore, to pray and pray through, it is important that such be done on the basis of the word of God. The Bible commands us in the scripture we read earlier by Moses admonishing his son Joshua that, "This book of the law shall not depart from your mouth." This implies that there is a need for us to allow the word of God to grow and gain strong roots in us so we can flourish in every area of our lives.

CONFESSION TO SLEEP

Confession on the word is another way one can apply the word of God when praying in thoughts. At a certain point in my prayer life, I was led by the Holy Spirit to confess the word from the innermost part of my heart to dwell on some key scriptures as I prepare to take my sleep. Sometimes, the urge would come brewing strong and welling up inside of me consequent on prior meditations of the word of God. These four powerful verses came from a previous study and they so intensely appealed to my sleep life even in their form and make up. When I stumbled on the scriptures and put them together, I suddenly felt I was going to be in for a real experience – Take a close look at them:

> "We having the same spirit of faith according as it is written, I believed, and therefore have I spoken; we also believe and therefore speak." (II Corinthians 4:13 KJV)

> "For by grace are ye saved through faith; and that not of yourself: it is the gift of God." (Ephesians 2:8 KJV)

> "And we have known and believed the love the God hath for us. God is love; and he that dwells in love dwells in God, and God in him." (I John 4:16 KJV)

> "Jesus said unto him, if you canst believe, all things are possible to him that believeth." (Mark 9:23 KJV)

The confessional recitation lines I came up with through the leading of the Holy Spirit was another channel of breakthrough I had with my praying in thoughts experience. This confession statement captures the truth embedded in the four mentioned scriptures above as it directly relates to my need.

It finally came out like this:

> *"By the mystery of the spirit of faith, which I have received by grace through faith, I have come to know and believe that all things are possible to them that believe to receive natural sleep and I take it now in Jesus Name."*

I would repeatedly recite this with my thoughts with so much care, faith and not forgetting to interject my regular hum at the specific time and intervals. The result of my confessions constantly reminds me of how powerful and mighty our God is in bringing my sleeplessness right down to its knees. The important thing however, is to understand the need to make sound confessional lines when attempting to put the method into practice. I will recommend for you to try my own, but if you feel confident of creating yours, it will be a fantastic achievement. All you need is to believe every word in it, commit it to memory and confess it **right in your thoughts** whenever you desire, make sure you stay still in your favorite sleeping position and watch what happens to your sleep.

PRAYING IN THE SPIRIT THROUGH PRAYING IN THOUGHTS

Praying in the Spirit is a communion done in tongues. It is a language of the Holy Spirit. Just as this is possible in verbal prayers, it is also possible to pray in the in our thoughts. At another point in my experience of praying in thoughts, I got elevated into a level of praying in the language of the Spirit in my heart and this actually ushered me into yet a new dimension of truth and power.

I find it important to share that the patterns of praying in thoughts being discussed in this book are not based on preference of which is more effective or not rather it is an exposition on the dimensions of engagement in regard to my personal choice per time. The aim is to bring people suffering from sleeplessness to the light of liberty and enjoy a whole new experience with God as each best suites anyone desiring of freedom.

When praying in the Spirit in our thoughts is consummated with accuracy, the potency of this level of this prayer cannot be denied. Without doubt, there is an unspeakable mystery in the workings of speaking in tongues. Apostle Paul writing in

(1Corinthians 14:2 NRSV) buttresses the point succinctly:

> "For those who speak in tongues do not speak to other people but to God; for nobody understands them, since they are speaking mysteries in the Spirit."

Personally, I see that the challenges i.e., insomnia, terminal ailments, poverty, demonic incursions etc. which we face as humans as some kinds of mysteries. The reason is the fact that we fail oftentimes to find an explanation on how they come to be. Going by this, I equally believe that since the cause of these defy our ability to understand or explain then there is no better way than tackling such with a superior mystery and this is where praying in the Spirit comes in.

I so much love the fact that praying in the Spirit is self-edifying and where Apostle Paul said, "Howbeit in the spirit" illuminated more on my revelation of praying in thoughts.

Paul again writing in the book of Jude 20 says:

> "But ye, beloved, building up yourselves on you most holy faith, praying in the Holy Ghost." kjv

Praying in the Spirit through my thoughts has been a life building experience, especially, when I consider how this has helped me in regaining my ability to get sleep. As a matter of fact, it consolidates the effectiveness of the aforementioned dimensions that validates the power of God's word as the source of this blessing. I have engaged in this countless times and as touching its working power, I am a living witness. The secret behind it is just simply believe, get filled, and continually rely on the Holy Spirit for strength to be steadfast in it.

Like I said earlier on, these patterns of praying in thoughts are not restricted to only insomnia victims (though this book is more focused on them); they are what a true child of God must possess. I have found them profound to a large extent as I cannot deny the transformation in my prayer life, in terms of passion, consistency and the desire to know the mind of God. This is my testimony.

Praying in thoughts is not defined by time; it is what can be done at any point in time. It is therefore a clarion call to all believers to rise up to also find access into this pattern of prayer in order to continue fulfilling the God-injunction of *"pray without ceasing"* in (1Thessalonians 5:17 KJV).

Praying in the Spirit in our thoughts is one sure way of achieving prayer without ceasing. I firmly believe that if the Children of God will ever fulfill this requirement, speaking in the sprit both audibly and from our thoughts should be considered into our prayer lives.

TRANSLATE AND TRANSPORT

The ability to change any form of thought of whatever nature to any of my praying in thoughts suggested remedies is a wonderful skill that must be known and mastered. It will interest you to know that this skill is easy and achievable. In reality, I can confidently assert that all that is required to achieve it is inbuilt in us by our maker and it is right within everyone who cares to discover and use it.

Transporting any form of thought from the head or (mind) to the heart is the secret behind getting easy sleep. This is a simple way of explaining what could be initially seen as a complicated concept. Let me quickly say here that it is a simple yet a delicate act. Living as a victim for a lengthy period of time afforded me more than ample moments to really dig deep into all I needed to know until I encountered the key that finally unlock the secret.

Complicated as the act may seem to suggest, the skill of mentally sieving and shifting one's thoughts from the realm of the brain region – where all thoughts are processed to the heart – where they are further internalized, caressed and retained also known as the province of emotional domain is a possibility by any human being. At this point, it is safe to conclude that this process is simple when we employ the required technique.

On any selected night, I can lie down to sleep and resolve to watch how my thoughts would be formed from my head or mind (whichever you choose to term it). Without any special knowledge of how the brain works, it is easy to notice especially for the victim of insomnia that the accumulated myriads of thoughts have the tendency to stick to the mind and would be reluctant to shift from there. What that literally implies is that a victim can spend minutes and even hours of random thoughts on all the subjects of choice. The distinct element of note here is that the accumulated thoughts would always reside on the mind, making it easy for the victim to transit from one event to another. Also, the automatic traffic flow of more unwelcomed thoughts to further keep the victim into deeper and longer periods of further needless thought activities. Overstressing the cumulative effect of the generated frustration resulting to this seemingly endless string of vain thought of the insomnia victim cannot be over emphasized.

While this may be the regular experience of one suffering from insomnia, it is hardly possible for such a person to visualize the existence of a thin line separation from that point of hopelessness to victory. It is also incredibly unthinkable to believe that just the knowledge of the skill of transporting the thought process along with the content retained in the head (mind), lies the ability to move the individual into the realm where when all the prescribed methods are effectively deployed could produce sleep at a rate unimaginable. This knowledge is critical to anyone who wishes to find the type of freedom I currently enjoy and I can encourage you to keep the determination until freedom is ensured.

Transporting the flow of ~~your~~ thoughts from your head to heart while ~~you are~~ trying to sleep is as easy as the act of breathing in and out. However, care must be the watchword. People who experience insomnia usually have to contend with a busy mind when they lay to sleep. As a routine, the sufferer has to find a way to be aware of exactly when the mind is prone to begin this process. At such point, victims will draw from within an inner energy to begin a self-determined translation of these obvious unwanted material thoughts into what is desired (using any praying in thoughts prescriptions). The process of such alteration can simply be achieved by instantaneously converting those thought contents which are not needed to those that generate sleep.

The process of thought transportation will not be complete until when the converted thoughts are moved from the point of conception to the emotional location. Naturally, thought processes begin from the mind and can be accumulated, stacked and kept there for as long as the individual desires. The beauty in the quality of shifting thoughts as early as possible from the mind to the emotional base which I see as the heart is the winning formula every insomnia victim must learn to have.

As a matter of my experience, when thoughts ~~enter~~ are finally moved to the heart, rather than keeping the body and mind alive by analyzing its content and fully conscious of the immediate environment as the case with the mind, the heart is by creation designed to caress and then have a form of deep interaction with the thought content independent of the mind. When this process is repeated and effectively consummated, the body by some unexplained spark of the infinite orchestration, will begin to gravitate towards a point where the whole process of thought generation becomes feeble and ineffective to carry out. What previously was considered to be an automatic process of unending flow of thoughts into the mind, begins to naturally collapse by itself. At this point pure natural sleep is already on the way.

A GOOD CONSCIENCE

In order to have a successful prayer life, the need for all forms of prayers and most importantly, the act of praying in thoughts with a good conscience is sacrosanct.

Overcoming insomnia would have remained a mirage for me if I had neglected this fundamental pillar ~~to~~ of praying in thoughts. I cannot count instances and situations where I had to battle to sleep when I was growing in the knowledge of this blessing without success. This, I did not realize until I came to the knowledge that carrying a heart laden with guilt to my sleep means I am not positioned for any result.

It is important to mention here that the imperative of having a good conscience before and during praying in thoughts as a praying lifestyle and to overcome sleeplessness cannot be over-emphasized. The fact is, until one, especially as a victim of insomnia, unbundles such things that are contrary unto God, getting a decent sleep is impossible. The Bible warns in the book of Proverbs:

> *"A man who refuses to admit his mistakes can never be successful. But if he confesses and forsakes them, he gets another chance"* (Proverbs 28:13 TLB).

After several attempts, I tried to overlook this disturbing trend to my sleep but I could not get past a period as I was so plagued by reoccurring failure of repeated loss of sleep. This, unfortunately, was as a result of some disturbing events in my life that brought guilt into my life, resulting to inability to sleep at that period. Of course, it was not too hard to figure out why it was so because after I had successfully dealt with the matter, it was not long that I recovered my ability to get sleep.

Why again having a good conscience is necessary for anybody to have a good sleep is because the feelings of approval and disapproval are all connected with the mind based on rights and wrongs. For this reason, the mind, being the ground of all the interplays of events that can lead to a sound or a distorted sleep, cannot harbor conflicts.

Although, a lot of people see the subject of having a good conscience strictly from a moral perspective, but as for me, I hold my stance from a spiritual point of view – and speaking from experience, a good conscience is indispensable to my sleep and general wellbeing.

As God's children, there is a need to bear in mind His ordinances in order to check whatever that may want to cause us to having and harboring a bad conscience which is inimical to getting blessed and overcoming life's challenges. We all, (most especially those who are desperate to overcome insomnia), must learn to do whatever it takes to imbibe the virtues of forgiveness, tolerance, kindness, and the ability to overlook offences. These and other qualities that can enhance their peace of minds have the capability of facilitating a healthy conscience – we must exhibit the fruit of the Spirit.

"But the fruit of the Spirit is love, joy, peace, longsuffering, gentleness, goodness, faith, meekness, temperance: against such there is no law." (Galatians 5:22-23 KJV)

It is through this (the fruit of the Spirit) that we are able to maintain effective communion and a constant relationship with God – our Father.

SUMMARY

Insomnia is not natural for a child of God, therefore, no thought should entertain it as such. It is an instrument of fear that has gained grounds but can be conquered by faith and steadfastness in God. The act of praying in thoughts is a confident assurance to overcome. To achieve results however is based on importunity (an intensified resolve to continue in faith and practice). Remember that only those who keep knocking the door get it opened (Matt 7:8). So, do not stop. Continue to push until something supernatural happens.

I am confident that by this revelation every sufferer of sleeplessness is liberated. Just a little faith is needed in this inspired activity of prayer and you will in no time find insomnia vanish from your life for good. Just have faith in Him and you live.

Finally, if you are reading this book and you have not given your life to Christ, I want to use this medium to invite you to meet with this Great God whom there is none like unto. He is the very source of victory over sleeplessness, a fulfilled life here on earth and a glorious one in the world to come.

Seek to know Him. Believe and accept that He sent His son Jesus Christ for the salvation of your soul. Surrender your heart to Him and ask Him to come in. He is more than willing to save and deliver you from every oppression of the devil. He is life eternal. John 3:16-17.

Go and be victorious

www.ingramcontent.com/pod-product-compliance
Lightning Source LLC
Chambersburg PA
CBHW031457040426
42444CB00007B/1132